Are you a Dragonfly?

For Kit – J.A.

For the Ladies of Holsworthy Library – T.H.

KINGFISHER
Kingfisher Publications Plc
New Penderel House
283–288 High Holborn
London WC1V 7HZ
www.kingfisherpub.com

First published by Kingfisher Publications Plc 2001

1 3 5 7 9 10 8 6 4 2

1TR/0201/TWP/GRS/150NYM

A CIP catalogue record for this book is available from
the British Library.

ISBN 0 7534 0540 7

Editor: Carron Brown
Series Designer: Jane Buckley

Printed in Singapore

Up the Garden Path

Are you a Dragonfly?

Judy Allen and Tudor Humphries

KING*f*ISHER

Are you a dragonfly?

If you are, your mother
laid her eggs in
the stems of
a water plant.

You swam out of one of them – and
so did lots of others just like you.

You are VERY small.

You are very hungry.
And – guess what –
you can breathe water
through the end of your tail.

Eat and grow.

Eat tiny water
creatures.

You have a special grabber for catching them. It's called a mask because it covers half your face.

Creep up on your prey –
then shoot out your mask
and grab it.

Eat and grow
until your skin
is so tight you
have to take it off.

Then eat and grow
some more and do it again.

8

And again.

And again.

Don't worry, there'll
always be a new
skin underneath.

9

Now you have
grown larger you
can eat larger food.
Try a tadpole – or a small fish.

Take care, though – there are plenty
who would like to eat YOU.
Beware of water beetles.
Water beetles

pounce!

Beware of ducks.
Ducks dive,
and they're
BIG.

Two years have passed. You're bored
with life in the water.

Crawl up a plant stem
into the air.

Do this at night so that birds
don't see you and eat you.

Hold on tight. As you dry out
your skin splits one more time.

Slowly, slowly,
climb out
of your
old skin.

First pull
your head free.
Next pull
your legs free.

Flop over backwards
and have a rest.

Now lean
forward, grab
your old skin
and pull your
whole body out.

Guess what – now
you can breathe air,
through tiny holes in
the sides of your body.

You're a dragonfly!

At first you're very
pale and crumpled.

But your beautiful
colours will come and
your two pairs of wings
will straighten out.

You're a brilliant flyer.

You can fly fast,

you can hover,

you can even
fly backwards.

You have
enormous eyes.
You can see all
around you, all the time.

You can see what's behind you,
in front of you, above you,
below you and beside you.

This is very useful
when you're looking for food.

This is also very useful when
you are dodging hungry birds
and avoiding spider's webs.

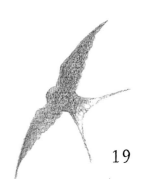

You were a fierce hunter
underwater – now you are
a fierce hunter in the air.

Hunt over ponds and streams
and slow-flowing rivers.
Hunt over moors and marshes
and neat hedgerows.

Hold your legs out in front
of you to catch your prey.

Hunt midges and mosquitoes,
flies, wasps and small butterflies.

When you've caught
something, eat it.

You are a hawker –
you hunt while you're flying.

This dragonfly is a darter –
it sits still until it sees its prey.
Then it darts out and grabs it.

This is not a dragonfly at all.
It's a damselfly. It's thinner and
lighter and slower than you.
It likes to pick small insects
off leaves and flowers.

Now look around you.
If you and all your friends look a bit
like this

or this

or this

you are not a
dragonfly.

You are...

...a human child.

You can't fly.

You can't breathe
underwater.

It's very unlikely that you have
a mask fixed to your face.

Never mind, you can do a great
many things a dragonfly can't.

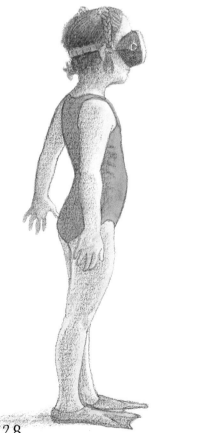

Also you don't have to
keep taking your skin off,
and you don't have to eat
midges and mosquitoes.

Best of all, you'll never, ever, EVER be eaten by a duck.

Did You Know...

...the dragonfly in this book is a
southern hawker, but there are more
than 4,800 different kinds
of dragonfly.

...dragonflies are
among the oldest of
the winged insects. They've been
on Earth for about 300 million
years – long before the dinosaurs.

...dragonflies have two pairs of wings and they can beat each pair separately, which is why they are such brilliant flyers.

...dragonflies usually rest with their wings spread out, but damselflies usually fold their wings above their backs, the way butterflies do.

31

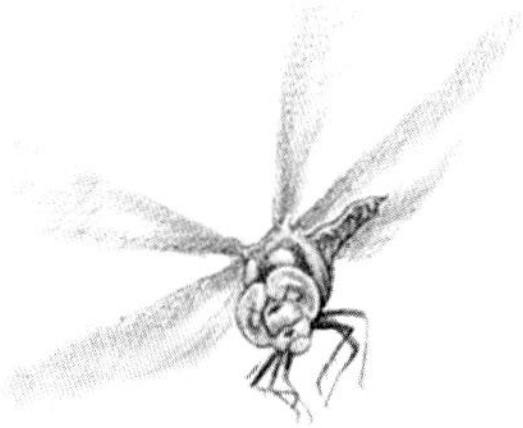